APPLE WATCH SERIES 5 FOR SENIORS

A RIDICULOUSLY SIMPLE GUIDE TO APPLE WATCH SERIES 5 AND WATCHOS 6

SCOTT LA COUNTE

RIDICULOUSLY SIMPLE BOOKS

ANAHEIM, CALIFORNIA

www.RidiculouslySimpleBooks.com

Copyright © 2019 by Scott La Counte.

All rights reserved. No part of this publication may be reproduced, distributed or transmitted in any form or by any means, including photocopying, recording, or other electronic or mechanical methods, without the prior written permission of the publisher, except in the case of brief quotations embodied in critical reviews and certain other noncommercial uses permitted by copyright law.

Limited Liability / Disclaimer of Warranty. While best efforts have been used in preparing this book, the author and publishers make no representations or warranties of any kind and assume no liabilities of any kind with respect to accuracy or completeness of the content and specifically the author nor publisher shall be held liable or responsible to any person or entity with respect to any loss or incidental r consequential damages caused or alleged to have been caused, directly, or indirectly without limitations, by the information or programs contained herein. Furthermore, readers should be aware that the Internet sites listed in this work may have changed or disappeared. This work is sold with the understanding that the advice inside may not be suitable in every situation.

Trademarks. Where trademarks are used in this book this infers no endorsement or any affiliation with this book. Any trademarks (including, but not limiting to, screenshots) used in this book are solely used for editorial and educational purposes.

Table of Contents

Introduction *10*
What's New In WatchOS 6 .... *11*
   What's New in WatchOS 6 11
So Many Models! What's Right for Me?! *16*
   Apple Watch Series 0 and 1 17
   Apple Watch Series 2 18
   Apple Watch Series 3 18
   Apple Watch Series 4 and 5 19
   Why pay more for steel 19
Will the Apple Watch Do This… *21*
   Things the Apple Watch won't do 22
   Apple Watch Without An iPhone Nearby 23
   Wi-Fi Without iPhone 23
   This and That 24
Okay, So How Do I Set This Thing UP? *26*
   Setting Things Up 27
Enough With the Setup! Show Me How to Use This Thing! *35*
   Power on, Wake, and Unlock 36

Adjusting Text Size, Brightness, Sounds, and Haptics 39
Charge the Apple Watch 42
Settings on the iPhone 44
Status Icons 46
Gestures and Shortcuts 49
Force Touch 53
Zooming 53
Turning off the Screen 54
Launching Siri 54
Locate your iPhone 54
Airplane Mode 54
Side Button 55
Last App 56
Apple Pay 56
Handoff Between the Apple Watch and iPhone 57
Arranging Icons 58
Installing Apps on The Watch 59
SOS 61
Noise 61
Breathe 63
Compass 63
Always On 64

Let's Make Faces…Apple Watch Faces, That Is! .. 65

Watch Faces and What They Do 67
    Activity Analog / Activity Digital 67
    Breathe 68
    California 69
    Mickey Mouse 69
    Toy story 70
    Gradient 70
    Meridan 71
    Modular / Modular Compact 71
    Motion 72
    Numerals / Numerals Duo / Numerals Mono 73
    Simple 73
    Solar 74
    Utility 74
    X-Large 75
    Chronograph 75
    Explorer 75
    Fire and Water 76
    Infograph / Infograph Modular 76
    Kaleidoscope 78
    Liquid Metal 78
    Pride / Pride Analog 78
    Astronomy 79
    Chronograph 79
    Color 80
    Siri 81
    Solar Dial 81
    Timelapse 82
    Photos 82

Show Me What This Watch Is Capable of…But Keep It Ridiculously Simple 86
    Messages 87
    Reading and Sending Email 91
    Managing Mail 92

- Flag an Email 92
- Mark as Unread 92
- Delete an Email 92
- Selecting the Inboxes that Appear 93
- Customize Alerts 93
- Message List 93

Siri 93

Making Phone Calls 94

Calendar 95
- Adding Events 96
- Responding to Event Invites 97

Reminders 97

Map 98
- Directions 99

Photos 100
- Pick an Album 100
- Storage 100

Camera Viewfinder 101

Music 102

Stocks 103

Weather 103

Activity 104

Workout 107

Check Your Heart Rate 109

Cycle Tracking 110

Set Alarms 112

Use a Timer 112

Use the Stopwatch 113

Audiobooks 114

Calculator 115

Remote Control 117
   Remote Play iTunes 117
   Remote for Apple TV 118

Walkie-Talkie 118

What Other Things Should I Know About the Apple Watch? 121

VoiceOver 122

Zoom 122

Bold Text 123

Handling 123
   Removing the Bands 123
   Band Care 124

A Little More Advanced 124
   Force Restarting the Apple Watch 124
   Resetting the Watch Settings 124
   Get Your Watch DNA 125
   Update Apple Watch Software 125

So Many Bands and Accessories, So Little Time. 126

Watch Bands & Accessories 126

Official Bands & Accessories 127
   Sport Band 127
   Classic Buckle 128
   Milanese Loop 128
   Modern Buckle 129
   Link Bracelet 130
   Leather Loop 131
   Apple Watch Magnetic Charging Cable 132

Accessibility.. *134*

About the Author *147*

Disclaimer: Please note, while every effort has been made to ensure accuracy, this book is not endorsed by Apple, Inc. and should be considered unofficial.

Introduction

The Apple Watch looks pretty snazzy, right? People have told you all about the cool features: like if you fall it will automatically call for help! They've told you about how you can send a text from your wrist. How you can even make a phone call.

That's all great. But how do you actually use it?!

As amazing as all the new features are, it's not quite as easy to use as an iPhone; the lack of buttons, the smaller screen, and general UI can make a frustrating initial experience.

It looks nothing like the iPhone or iPad interface you are used to--except for a handful of icons. If you are lost and don't have a lot of time to comb through thousands of pages of tech-speak just to learn how to use a watch, then this book is for you!

This book is based on the book "The Ridiculously Simple Guide to Apple Watch Series 5" but includes sections specifically for seniors (including accessibility features that make text easier to see).

Are you ready to start enjoying your new Apple Watch? Then let's get started!

[1]
What's New In WatchOS 6

> This chapter will cover:
> - New and updated features

WatchOS 6 is the latest operating system available for Apple Watch. You can update any older generation Apple Watch to this operating system except the original watch (also known as Series 0).

What's New in WatchOS 6

Looks-wise, WatchOS 6 doesn't look that much different from other WatchOS's.

What's changed is more in terms of added features and refinements to apps that are already there.

In the past, you would need to install watch apps on your phone, and then put them on your watch. In WatchOS 6, there is now a native app store. That means you can download apps directly from your watch. Of course, you can also continue to do it the previous way as well.

In terms of new features, there are a few of note:

1. A Noise App – This app measures the noise of an environment and warns you when prolonged periods in that setting can damage your ears.
2. Cycle Tracking App – This app lets women keep track of their menstrual cycle.
3. Calculator – Surprisingly, Apple Watch has been without one for some time, and users had to rely on third parties to get one.
4. Compass App – A new digital compass has been added to the watch (Series 5 only).
5. Audiobooks and Voice Memos – These are basically versions of their iPhone companions.
6. Messages – Messages has been on the watch from the start, but the latest version lets you send the newest Animoji and Memoji stickers.

7. Reminders – Apple refined their Reminders app on the iPhone and that design is put in watch form on OS 6.
8. Voice Memos – Record memos to your watch with this new watch app.

If you have a MacBook with your Apple Watch, Apple has added a new security feature that lets you unlock your computer from your watch.

Apple has also added new watch faces, which will be covered later in this book.

[2]
So Many Models! What's Right for Me?!

> This chapter will cover:
> - What's the difference between all the series of watches?
> - Why pay more for steel?
> - What's the right model for me?

The Apple Watch comes in several different Series. Every watch—from the original Apple Watch to the Series 5—are compatible with any previous generation band. So, if you have an original Apple Watch, you can still use that expensive band you may have picked up. You can also find third-party bands much cheaper on Amazon and other online retailers.

The Milanese Loop band from Apple, for example, retails for $149; the below example looks the same but is less than $20! The quality is not the same, but if you just want something that looks nice, then this could be a good option. I'll cover bands in greater detail at the end of this book.

Each version of the watch comes in two sizes: 38mm and 42mm on earlier models, and 40mm and 44mm for Series 4 and 5. Each version also comes in aluminum and stainless steel—stainless steel is the most expensive.

Apple Watch Series 0 and 1

The Apple Watch is the watch that started everything; there was no "Series" number—so when you see Apple Watch Series 1, you aren't actually looking at the first edition of the watch.

This year is the first year that the original Apple Watch did not receive a WatchOS update (that means the people who paid upwards of $20,000 for a watch, now have a worthless piece of technology). It still works fine—it just doesn't have new features. You can't find it new anymore, but you probably can find a used one in decent shape for the low $100s.

The Apple Watch Series 1 is still supported (though it probably won't be next year) and you can get it certified refurbished on the Apple Store website starting at $169.

Apple Watch Series 2

The Series 2 introduced water resistance and GPS to the watch. You might occasionally see it pop up on the Apple Refurbished store, but it is no longer sold new.

Apple Watch Series 3

Cellular was added to the Apple Watch Series 3. That means you can make calls from your watch even if your phone is nowhere nearby. It is currently the cheapest watch you can buy new at $199.

Apple Watch Series 4 and 5

You can't buy the Series 4 new directly from Apple; any you see in stores are last year's models. They're great watches, but unless you find a remarkable deal on them somewhere, you should stick with the current model: the Series 5.

The Series 5 watch starts at $399. The biggest noticeable difference from older phones is cosmetic: it's bigger than previous generations, and yet it's also thinner and lighter. On the inside the processor is faster, the screen is brighter, and the battery lasts longer.

The Series 5 Apple Watch is considered the ultimate watch in fitness. It's also the watch you'll want to get your elderly parents and grandparents—it has drop detection and will automatically call for help if it detects you've fallen and don't respond.

Why pay more for steel

Which watch is right for you? If you have an itching to spend $1k+ for a watch, then you are probably considering the steel model with Hermes band over the sports model. What's the difference? In terms of wear and tear, both watches will hold up pretty well; every watch—even the more expensive ones—have the same hardware. The steel model has a stronger display that is slightly more scratch-resistant.

Unlike the iPhone or iPad, you aren't paying more for more memory—you are paying for the finish—so it's really a question of taste. The steel watch is slick, smooth and shiny. If you can afford it and want something a little classier, then the steel watch is a good option.

If you are trying to decide between the Series 1 and Series 2, it really comes down to how you will use it. If you're a swimmer and want to use your watch in the pool, then you definitely want the Series 2 and up; the GPS on Series 2 is also great for fitness and tracking where you go when your phone isn't next to you. Series 1 (and even the original Apple Watch) is still an excellent watch, however.

If you are trying to decide if you should buy the Series 3 or 5, my recommendation is to spend a little more for the 5. It will be supported by WatchOS the longest. The largest display will also work better with newer apps being built for the watch, and it will likely be supported longer.

Also, if you already have the watch and don't like the band, you are able to return the band (even if it's opened) to any Apple Store within 14 days for a band of equal value. (Note: this offer will not necessarily run forever, so check with your local store before going in for an exchange.)

[3]
Will the Apple Watch Do This…

> This chapter will cover:
> - What the Apple Watch won't do
> - What the Apple Watch will do without an iPhone nearby
> - What the Apple Watch will do on Wi-Fi without an iPhone nearby
> - This and that

When you think about the watch, you might have certain expectations—perhaps it's watching Netflix from your wrist or FaceTime with your friends. So before continuing to how the watch works, let me cover really quickly the major things the watch cannot do (that some people think it can)—and what it can do.

Things the Apple Watch won't do…
- Play videos; it can render very small clips, but don't plan on watching *The Lord of the Rings* on your wrist.
- Type messages; there is no onboard keyboard…just a microphone. You can scribble to type (we'll cover that later).
- Play games; while Apple Watch games do exist, the watch is a companion to the phone, and meant for viewing short messages…not playing games. So yes, you can play games, but this is not what you want to get to meet your gaming needs.
- Sync with non-Apple phones; the Apple Watch will not work with any phone but iPhone.
- Work with older phones; the Apple Watch is for iPhone 5 and up.
- Work with traditional headphones; there's no audio input on the Apple Watch. It does work with Bluetooth headphones, but these are not included with the watch.
- Take a photo; you can view photos on the watch—you can even use it as an external viewfinder to take a photo on your iPhone—but the watch has no built-in camera.

Apple Watch Without An iPhone Nearby

To be entirely clear, you must own an iPhone to use the Apple Watch. The watch is not compatible with Android or any other smartphone. But you don't have to take your iPhone everywhere to use the watch. And if you have cellular on the watch, there's more you can do here without your phone nearby. Here are some of the things you can do if you don't have your phone nearby:

- Set the time.
- Play music (you can put up to 2 GB of songs on your watch…to put it another way, that's about 500 songs).
- Track your run / exercise—it will keep a record of things like calories burned, heart rate, and distance / pace, and then sync it to your phone when you have it nearby again.
- Track your standing time and steps.
- See your photos—75 MB is reserved for photos.
- Read, delete and flag email that has come in.
- Use the alarm, stopwatch, and timer.
- Use Passbook to show tickets (like an airplane or concert ticket).
- Use Apple Pay to buy things.

Wi-Fi Without iPhone

And here's what you can do if you don't have your phone, but you do have Wi-Fi:

- Send and receive text messages and use digital touch messages (i.e. drawing and tapping patterns to send as a message).
- Use Siri.

This and That

A few other things you might need to know about the watch…

- It takes about two hours to fully charge your Apple Watch.
- It takes your iPhone's battery…kind of; because the watch talks to your phone, your phone's battery will be used. It's not significant, but it's enough that you might notice 30 minutes to an hour of usage gone by the end of the day that used to be there.
- There's a feature on the device called "Taptic Engine"—fancy sounding, right? But what is it? The Taptic Engine lets you receive feedback on your wrist that feels like someone is tapping you.
- You can use it as a phone…sort of. Yes, it sounds very Dick Tracy-like to get phone calls on your wrist, but don't get too excited—it's a little awkward to use; to get the most out of it, you really need to put it up to your mouth. And the audio that comes out of the speakers is subpar at best.
- It tells time! Well yes—you probably knew that. But it also tells time very precisely

(within 50 milliseconds), which makes it one of the most accurate watches ever made.

[4]
Okay, So How Do I Set This Thing Up?

> This chapter will cover:
> - Setting up the Apple Watch for the first time
> - Restoring from a previous generation Apple Watch

This chapter is all about taking it out of the box and setting it up for the first time. You might be perfectly comfortable doing this without reading how. If that's the case, then skip ahead to the next chapter—you won't miss anything here.

The process is pretty simple, but if you want an explanation of what it's actually doing in each step—like why it asks about privacy—then read on.

NOTE TO USERS UPDATING: If you are updating your iPhone and watch from a previous OS, there's a chance you will have to reformat your watch to get it to sync. If that happens, then from your watch you need to go to Settings > General > Reset; next tap Erase All Content and Settings.

Setting Things Up

Once you have the watch out of the box, push the side button to turn it on. You get the following screen:

Because the Apple Watch has no keyboards, setup is a bit unusual compared to other Apple products. Setup for the watch actually begins not with the watch, but with the iPhone.

If you aren't running iPhone iOS 12 and up, then the first thing you need to do is update your phone. You also need at least an iPhone 5—anything less will not be compatible. To see if your phone needs to be updated, go to Settings on the iPhone, then General, and finally Software Update—it will tell you if your phone is up-to-date.

If you are up-to-date on everything, then go to the Watch app, and tap Start Pairing. This gives you the below setup screen.

Place your watch (make sure it's turned on) within that square box. You'll notice your watch has a moving image on its screen now. In just a few seconds, it will say your watch is paired.

From here you can either Restore from a backup or Set Up as a new watch. If you've never owned an Apple Watch (or you want to start fresh), then select the second choice. If you've owned previous generations, then select the first (this will put all your preferences from your old watch on your new watch). Assuming you are setting it up as a new watch, the next screen will ask if you are wearing the watch on your left or right wrist. Based on your answer, the orientation of the watch will change (you can change this later).

30 | *Apple Watch Series 5 For Seniors*

Next you'll need to agree to the terms. Feel free to read it thoroughly through—then give it to your lawyer to ask what they think...or just hit Agree like everyone else. After you agree to the terms, you'll get a message telling you some apps will use things like your location. That sounds scary, but what it basically means is if you want to use a map to get directions, then it has to know where you are first. Your only option here is to hit OK.

Scott La Counte | 31

After you agree to share your location with apps, you need to add a passcode. This works much like your phone (before your phone had fingerprint to unlock or Face ID). You don't have to add a passcode. Adding it protects your watch from someone stealing it and then using it.

Is Apple breaking your heart with this setup? The next screen will help detect it! It tells you all about the new heart monitor feature. Read it and then hit Continue.

Next is SOS. This feature will text your contacts to tell them if you are in trouble. It's sort of like Apple's version of "I've fallen and I can't get up." Read it and hit Continue to proceed.

You may not have known it, but a lot of your favorite apps already have Watch apps. You can add everything that you already own, or pick and choose them later. Personally, I would be careful of selecting all of them. This is the easiest option, but you'll probably find a lot of your favorite phone apps are sort of pointless on your wrist.

You're just about done. Your phone and watch are now syncing with all the settings you just selected. If you decided to install all apps, it will take a few minutes to finish. Along the way you'll probably also get a message about your phone and watch now sharing text messages—that just means if someone texts you, you'll get it on your wrist too.

A message will now appear on both your phone and watch saying it's done. You can now use your watch!

[5]
ENOUGH WITH THE SETUP! SHOW ME HOW TO USE THIS THING!

This chapter will cover:
- Adjusting settings
- What status icons represent
- Force Touch
- Gestures and shortcuts
- Arranging icons
- Handoff between Apple Watch and iPhone

Setup is pretty self-explanatory, right? What you *really* are waiting for is how to use this thing! So let's get started!

Power on, Wake, and Unlock

To turn your watch on, press and hold the side button until the Apple logo appears; to turn it off press and hold the side button until a slider appears telling you to drag it to the right to power off.

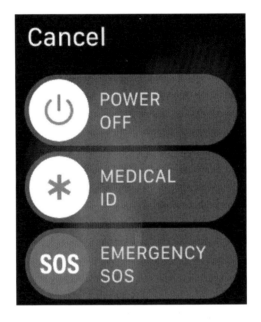

Taking your watch off standby is the most seamless thing you'll do—just lift your wrist! How's that for easy? Turning standby back on is just as simple—put your wrist down.

If you lift your wrist and standby doesn't turn off, then it's possible that you changed a setting. Open the Settings button on the Home screen of your watch (it looks just like the one on your phone except it's round), and then go to General and Orientation—make sure Orientation is set to the wrist that you wear—if you are wearing it on your right hand and Orientation is set to left hand, for example, then change it. The other thing that might have happened is your battery has drained.

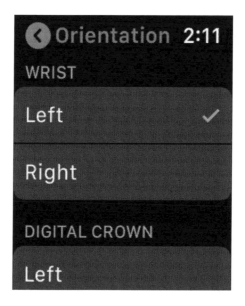

When you lift your wrist, the watch will either show your watch face (i.e. time) or the last app opened. By default it shows the watch face, but if you want it to go to your last activity, then go to Settings, then General, and finally Wake Screen—once you tap this, pick Resume Previous Activity.

38 | *Apple Watch Series 5 For Seniors*

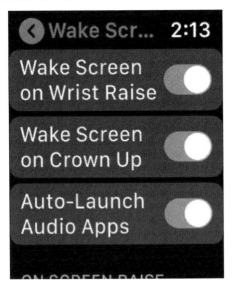

You also have the ability to unlock the watch with your phone using a passcode. This is a great feature if you take your watch off a lot. It doesn't mean you need to put in a passcode every time you look at the time—it only needs it when the watch is off your wrist or being worn too loosely. The passcode can be the same as the phone, but it's recommended that the code is different. To activate Passcode, go to Settings from your watch's Home screen, and then scroll down until you see Passcode, then tap it. Tap Turn on Unlock with iPhone. If you ever want to change it, just follow the same steps, but pick Change Passcode.

If you ever forget your passcode, then unpair your watch from the iPhone and erase all the settings.

Adjusting Text Size, Brightness, Sounds, and Haptics

I hope you love settings, because that's where we'll stay for this section!

The Apple Watch is probably smaller than you're used to when reading messages, emails, news, etc.; if it's too small then you can make text larger by going to Brightness and Text Size, tap Text Size and then use the Digital Crown knob to increase or decrease it. You can also check or uncheck making the text boldface. (Note: before boldface is in place, the watch will need to be reset.)

From this same menu, you can adjust how bright the watch is.

If you don't like the default sounds on your watch, then go to Sounds & Haptics from the Settings menu. Use your Digital Crown knob to adjust how loud it gets. You can also mute sounds by switching to Silent mode. (Note: muting does not turn off sound on alarms.)

Scott La Counte | 41

If you scroll just a little more to the bottom, one fun option is the Tap to Speak Time for the Mickey Mouse watch display (only for this display). When this is on, anytime you tap the Mickey Mouse display, Mickey's voice will tell you the time. I'll cover how to change displays later in this book.

For some notifications, you will get a tap on your wrist, which you may love or hate. If you hate it, then go back to the previous menu. Next, go to the Haptic section and you can toggle it on or off—and also make it more prominent.

Charge the Apple Watch

Charging your watch is very simple; it might be a little strange at first, because the charger is magnetic and doesn't plug into the watch—rather it snaps into the back. Make sure you use the charger that came with your device—using any other might overcharge the device, which will drain the battery quickly.

It takes about two hours to fully charge the watch.

If you want to know how much time is needed for a full charge, swipe up from the watch face, which brings up Glances, and then swipe to the Battery glance.

When the watch has less than 10% power left, it will automatically go into a Power Reserve mode—in this mode, the watch will show the time, but other apps won't be available. You can also manually turn Power Reserve on by pressing the side button for three seconds until the Power menu comes up, then swiping Power Reserve.

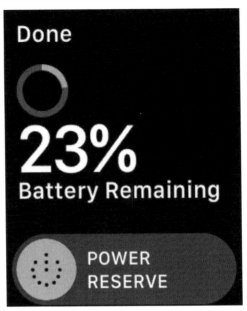

You can see how much time you have left in your battery reserve at any time by swiping up from the watch face to bring up Glances, then swiping to Power Reserve. You can also use the Apple Watch app on your iPhone to see the last time you charged it.

NOTE: Anytime I mention Glances in this book, that just means swipe up from your devices—there are a lot of Glances I'll be covering.

Settings on the iPhone
Now that we covered all the settings, here's a hint you'll probably be annoyed I didn't tell you about earlier: you can do all of this on your phone!

You don't always have your phone on you, so you should know where they are on both the watch and the phone. Most people will find it easier to control settings on a larger device, however.

To adjust the settings, go to your Watch app on the phone, and then scroll down to the setting you want. Anything you change here will sync to your watch automatically. There's nothing else to do!

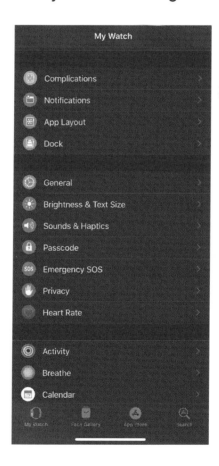

Status Icons

Notifications on the Apple Watch come in many forms; one way is through status icons; these icons let you quickly glance down at your wrist and know there's a new email or your watch needs to be charged. Some are less obvious than others. The status icons and what they mean are listed below:

You have an unread notification such as an email.

The Apple Watch is charging.

Your battery is low.

The Apple Watch is locked and needs a passcode to use.

Your watch is in Do Not Disturb mode and will not make any sounds or light up until enabled again; alarms, however, will still work.

The Apple Watch is in Airplane mode and only non-wireless features work—Bluetooth and Wi-Fi are not turned on.

Your watch is in Theater mode and stays silent and the screen stays dark, unless you tap on the screen or press one of the buttons.

Your watch is connected to a Wi-Fi network instead of your phone.

This is something you'll only see on an Apple Watch with a cellular connection. It indicates you are connected to cellular; the bars indicate how strong the connection is. Four is the highest.

Again, this is only something you'll see on an Apple Watch with a cellular connection, and it means you have lost your cellular connection.

If you are swimming or doing something with lots of water, this indicates that water lock is on, and the watch will not respond to taps.

Swipe up to your Glances and you'll see this icon; it represents your audio connection. Tapping on this will let you switch audio from your watch to another device. So, for instance, if you are listening to music and want it to play on a wireless headset.

Location service is on. What does this mean? It means there's an app (such as Maps) that's using your location in the background.

Your watch is no longer paired with your phone.

There's wireless activity happening or some other kind of active event—an app loading, for example.

If you are using the Workout app, then you'll see this status icon appear. Tap it to switch back to the app.

I'll cover the Walkie-Talkie feature later; for now, just understand that this icon represents that feature.

You'll see this icon when audio is playing.

Gestures and Shortcuts

With such a limited space, Apple really made use of something called Gestures. Gestures is essentially your watch doing different things based on how you touch or swipe the watch. If you have an iPhone or Mac with Force Touch, you'll be somewhat familiar with this. If not, don't worry—it's easy to understand.

This section will give you a quick overview of the gestures and shortcuts that let you do what you need to do quickly.

The Big Three

There are three actions that you'll use more than others.

#1

The one shortcut you will use the most is the Digital Crown knob; pressing it will always get you back to the Home screen. It's like the Home button on your iPhone (if you have an iPhone that still has a Home screen button).

#2

Swiping down from the top edge of your watch face will get you notifications. If you missed a text, email or any other alert, then swipe down and you can see what it was. You probably know this gesture is exactly the same as your iPhone—Apple, whenever possible, tries to keep gestures the same or similar.

If you swipe left over a notification, you'll get two more options: clear and more options.

Clear does exactly what it sounds like—it clears! More options lets you change how a notification is delivered.

Notifications can start adding up really quickly. Maybe you are the type who loves to go through each one and clear them individually; I find it time-consuming and would rather clear them at once. That's easy! Just firm press on any notification (that means you touch it firmly and hold until a message pops up). When the Clear All message comes up, tap it. This won't delete the message—only the notification.

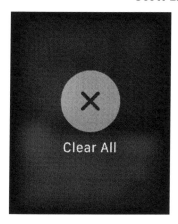

#3

Swipe up from the bottom edge of your watch face to see Glances. Glances is a little like the Control Center on your iPhone—on older iPhones it's the same gesture to get there (swiping up); newer iPhones access this by swiping down at the upper right corner.

Glances are nothing more than shortcuts and toggles. All those status icons I just mentioned? A lot of them are turned on here.

So when you want Swim mode or Airplane mode turn on, for example, just go into Glances and push the button. Push it again to turn it off. Some of the icons (like the battery percent icon) will open up more options.

One status icon not covered previously was the flashlight, which is one of the Glance options. On your iPhone, the flashlight is pretty useful (and bright); on the watch? Not so much. On the watch, the display turns on, so you have "some" light, but it's not the same brightness as using your camera's flash like on the phone. Swiping up will bring up the different kinds of flashlights (white, flashing white, and red). To turn it off, swipe down.

At the bottom of Glances, there's an Edit button. If you tap that, you'll be able to drag and drop icons around (you can't delete them); this way you can organize the icons in order of the ones you use the most.

Force Touch

Force Touch measures not just what you are touching, but how hard you are touching it. On your watch / clock screen, pressing a little harder on the screen will let you change the watch face. In apps, Force Touch is used a bit like right-clicking on a computer—it brings up options.

Zooming

You may be used to pinching and zooming on your iPhone and iPad; be prepared to be disappointed...on a smaller screen this method just doesn't work. In its place is the Digital Crown, which can be used to zoom in and out by turning the knob. You can use it to magnify things like photos and maps.

Turning off the Screen

There's no physical button to turn off the Apple Watch. To turn the screen off you can either put your hand down or cover the watch with your other hand. You can also silence alarms by covering your hand over the screen.

Launching Siri

There are two quick ways to launch Siri: one, press and hold the Digital Crown; two, lift up your wrist and speak—no buttons are required. Previously, you'd have to say "Hey Siri"; that's no longer needed. The watch can detect you lifting your wrist to speak, and hears what you say.

Locate your iPhone

If you can't find your iPhone, you can quickly ping it with your watch to see if it's nearby. Go to your watch face, swipe up to bring up Glances, then tap the Phone icon.

This will make your phone start beeping. (Note: for this to work you must enable Find My iPhone from iCloud.)

Airplane Mode

Most airlines will let you leave your watch on while you're flying, but they will want it in Airplane mode (which turns off settings that might interfere with the plane).

To put the watch in Airplane mode, go to your watch face, swipe up from the bottom to bring up Glances, and go to the Settings glance, then tap the button that looks like an airplane. Repeat the steps to turn the mode off.

If you'd like the watch to go in Airplane mode whenever your phone does, then go to the Apple Watch app, tap My Watch, then tap Airplane mode and turn on Mirror iPhone. Repeat the steps to disable.

Side Button

To toggle between your most recently used apps, press the side button on from the watch face. This brings up all the apps like a rolodex.

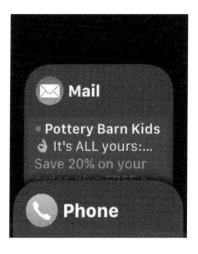

Use the Digital Crown to scroll through them; tap once to open an app; swipe right to crash the app.

Last App

Need to go back to the last app used quickly? Double click the Digital Crown.

Apple Pay

To use Apple Pay, double tap the side button; it will come up with your credit card and tell you to put it near the reader (your phone does not need to be nearby); once it is by the reader you enter your passcode. Worried about someone taking your watch and using your credit card? It won't work when it's taken off your wrist.

If you want to use a different credit card, swipe to the left. When you find the card you want, turn it to face the reader. When the transaction goes through, you'll hear a beep and you'll feel a tap—this alerts you to the fact that the transaction is complete.

Before you can use Apple Pay, however, you need to set it up. This is done on the iPhone. From your iPhone, tap the Apple Watch app, and then scroll to Add Credit or Debit Card, and then tap it. You can either use a card on file with iTunes or add a new card. In either case, you'll have to add your security number (or the full number if you are adding a new card); depending on the card, you may need to verify with another step, which is usually a text message with a code from your bank. When you get the code, just tap Verify and enter it. You're all set to use your watch to buy things!

Handoff Between the Apple Watch and iPhone

Handoff lets you toggle between your watch and your phone without losing your place. If you are reading an email on your watch, and want to reply on your phone, then go to Handoff on your phone. Handoff used to appear on the Lock screen—it's a little less obvious now. You now access Handoff from your app switcher screen on the iPhone (see below).

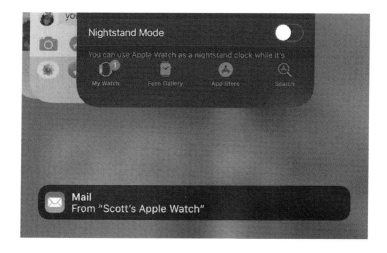

On a MacBook, Handoff is in the dock.

You can turn Handoff on and off by opening the Apple Watch app on your iPhone, going to My Watch, then tapping on General, and Enable Handoff.

Arranging Icons

Arranging icons on the watch isn't that much different from arranging them on your iPhone or iPad. To start, go to your Home screen, then touch and hold an app icon; you can now drag it to a new location.

To install a new app, open the Apple Watch app from your iPhone, and then tap the App Store to find apps for the Apple Watch. Once you download them to your phone, you'll see a message on your watch asking if you want to install them. Just tap yes and you are done. When you are on the normal App Store, you'll see a little round icon and "Offers Apple Watch App" if it's an app with a companion app for the watch.

The watch doesn't have as much room as your phone, so you might run out of space. To view how much storage is being used by an app, go to the Apple Watch app on the iPhone, then tap on My Watch, then go to General and Usage. Finally, view the storage being used by each app.

If you would like to remove an app, go to the Home screen on the watch, then tap and hold the app you want to remove; when an 'x' appears over the app, tap it. It will remain installed on your iPhone unless you remove it from there as well. Apps that were installed by Apple (such as the Settings button) cannot be removed.

If you find the screen a bit too small for rearranging icons, then you can also do it right from your iPhone; just open the Apple Watch app, tap the My Watch tab, and tap Layout. You rearrange the icons just as you would on your watch.

Installing Apps on The Watch

The days of using your phone to find and download apps are over with OS 6. True, you can still use the method referenced in the above section, and you may actually prefer it because it's easier to navigate and browse.

To find apps directly on your watch and skip the old method, open the Apps app on your watch.

This brings up a watch version of the App Store; you can either search for apps or use the Digital Crown to look through featured apps.

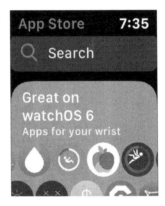

When you see an app that you want, tap it, then tap the Get button.

SOS

SOS allows your watch to call local emergency services to tell them your location; this is obviously something you only use in an emergency—it's not something to try out just to see how it works! To enable it, hold the side button for three seconds, and then swipe SOS.

Noise

Series 4 and up watches will have a new app appear after updating to OS 6: the Noise app.

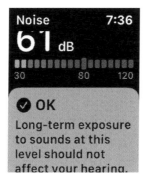

The Noise app uses the microphone in your watch to measure the sound levels of your environment. When it raises to a level that can harm your hearing, it can notify you.

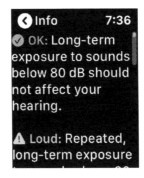

To turn it on, open the app and select enable.

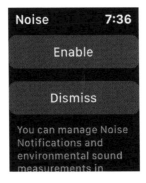

Once it's turned on, you can open it at any time to measure the sound level. You can also adjust when you get notifications about the sound levels by going into Settings on your watch, then Noise, then Notifications.

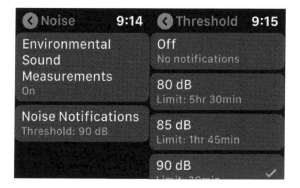

Breathe

Breathe introduced on the WatchOS 3 home screen. It's a free relaxation app designed to help calm your body after a workout or stressful day at work.

Compass

The Series 5 watch is very similar to the Series 4; there are a few things that make it unique. One exclusive app is the Compass.

The compass is pretty much what you would expect: it shows the direction the watch is facing along with the current location and elevation. You can use the Digital Crown to see your incline and other coordinates. Firmly pressing on the display will let you edit your bearings.

Always On

When people talk about the differences between the Series 5 and older models, they will probably cite the always-on display. On older watches, the display turns off as soon as you set your wrist down. Most people with the Series 5 will probably want to keep it on; there might be settings where you'd like it turned off, however. To turn it off, go to the Settings app on the watch, tap Display & Brightness, then tap Always On. You can also use this Settings screen to hide sensitive notifications—such as calendar events and messages.

[6]
LET'S MAKE FACES...APPLE WATCH FACES, THAT IS!

This chapter will cover:
- What is an Apple Watch face?
- How to change the Apple Watch face
- How to customize different Apple Watch faces

The Apple Watch has dozens of different faces to pick from—from traditional to modern to even a cute Mickey Mouse (and Minnie Mouse, of course). To change the watch's face, place your finger firmly over the current face for three seconds. The face will zoom back and you can swipe back and forth across your watch's screen to see different faces.

When you find the face that you want, tap it. Before tapping, however, you can also customize it by tapping the Customize button.

You'll see dots at the top of the screen to indicate how much you can change. On the first screen, scroll with the knob to see what changes (it might, for instance, change the amount of numbers on the watch). When you are done, swipe across the screen to get to the next customizable screen: colors. Using the knob, you can scroll through all of the colors. Swipe again, and you'll be at a screen that lets you add the current weather, calendar, etc. You'll tap on the screen to change any of these features, but first you have to swipe the off to on.

After you have customized the face to suit your needs, press the knob. This will bring you back to the main face screen. From here, tap the face.

Your new face should now appear with all its customizations. If you added options for calendar and weather, you can now tap those options to bring up more detailed views. To bring up the more detailed view, tap your finger on the icon on the screen (e.g., to see the weather, tap the weather icon).

And remember, anytime you want to know the time anywhere else in the world, just lift your wrist and say, "What time is it in...?"

Watch Faces and What They Do

Every face has different details that can be added or removed. Below is a list of the current watch faces and what you can add to them. Watch faces that have status icons can be touched to load the associated app. (Note: not all of these faces will be on earlier watch models; additionally, some are only available to watch models with cellular.)

You may notice that many of the faces below don't show up when you firm press to change the watch face. That's because only the most common ones appear. Swiping all the way over brings up New; tap that, and then use the Digital Crown to scroll through all the other faces.

Activity Analog / Activity Digital

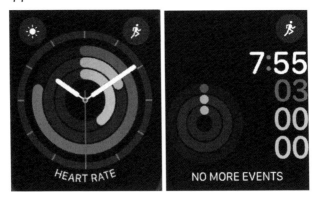

This is the face to use when working out. It measures your progress but has an overlay of a clock to give you the time as well. There are two versions: analog with no numbers; and digital with numbers.

Breathe

Unleash the yogi inside you. This simplistic watch face has one goal: encouraging you to breathe.

California

California turns your face into a more traditional watch face. There are lots of customizations here; you can go from full screen to a circular face, for example, by going into customizations, then turning your Digital Crown on the full screen menu.

Mickey Mouse

Featuring Mickey Mouse (and now Minnie Mouse), this is certainly the most whimsical and animated watch experience. Tap him and he will speak the time—if sound is on. The following can be added to the face: date, calendar, moon phase, sunrise / sunset, weather, activity summary, alarm, timer, stopwatch, battery charge, world clock, and stocks.

Toy story

Not to be outdone by the Mickey face, is the Toy Story face. Tap the screen to get a different animation.

Gradient

Gradient is a very simple face that will slightly change as time passes.

Meridan

A classic look with four subdials.

Modular / Modular Compact

A very modern-looking face with lots of room to add things. Color can be adjusted, and the following features can be added: calendar, moon phase, sunrise /sunset, weather, stocks, activity summary, alarm, timer, stopwatch, battery charge, world clock. There are two versions of this face: Modular and Modular Compact.

Motion

This is one of the few Apple Watch faces that is fully animated. You can pick between a butterfly, flower, and jellyfish. The following can be added to the face: date.

Numerals / Numerals Duo / Numerals Mono

Numerals has three unique designs (normal, Duo, and Mono) with several customizations. The basic design shows the time in a bold and easy to read way.

Simple

As the name implies, this is the simplest classic watch face. The following can be adjusted on the face: color of the sweep hand and the numbering of the dial. The following can be added: date, calendar, moon phase, sunrise / sunset, weather, activity summary, alarm, timer, stopwatch, battery charge, and world clock.

Solar

Bring out your inner scientist with this face, which displays the sun's position in the sky.

Utility

A very basic and classic looking face; the following features can be changed: the color of the second hand and the numbering on the dial. The following can be added to the face: date, calendar, moon phase, sunrise / sunset, weather, activity summary, alarm, timer, stopwatch, batter charge, world clock, and stocks.

X-Large

X-Large is the most simplistic modern face—it's also the boldest looking. The following can be adjusted: color.

Chronograph

Measures the exact time in increments.

Explorer

This face is a cellular exclusive. The goal of the watch face is to show you the cell signal strength.

Fire and Water

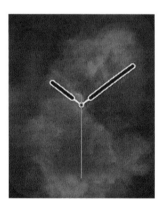

Animates with smoke whenever you lift it.

Infograph / Infograph Modular

This was an Apple Watch Series 4 exclusive face; it gives you a wealth of info at your wrist—time in another city, UVI index, weather, etc.

If you updated your watch or got a new one, then you might be a bit surprised to see it's now a B&W face. Not to worry! Color is still there and it's a quick fix—just press and hold, then select customize, then use your Digital Crown to scroll to Multicolor, then press your Digital Crown twice.

Kaleidoscope

The face changes patterns based on your preferences.

Liquid Metal

Animates with melting metal whenever you lift your wrist.

Pride / Pride Analog

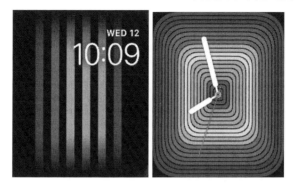

Celebrating Pride colors has long been a face on the Apple Watch; starting with OS 6 a new analog face is included.

Astronomy

This watch face shows you the exact position of different planets and displays day, date and time.

Chronograph

A very precise and classic watch face that includes a stopwatch that can be activated from the watch face. The following can be adjusted: dial details and face color. You can also add the following to the face: date, moon phase, sunrise / sunset, calendar, weather, stocks, activity summary, alarm, timer, battery charge, and world clock.

Color

A very basic face whose primary feature is to change colors. The following can be adjusted: dial color. The following can be added to the face: date, moon phase, sunrise / sunset, weather, activity summary, stopwatch, timer, battery charge, world clock, and your monogram.

Siri

The Siri face doesn't look like what you might expect; you think Siri and you might think of those waves that appear when you say "Hey Siri"; the watch face takes a look at your day (like your calendar appointments, traffic and weather) and displays it in an organized way; you can turn your Digital Crown to see more events.

Solar Dial

This face features a 24-hour dial that tracks the sun; the dial (either analog or digital) moves opposite the suns path.

Timelapse

Features time-lapse videos that change from morning, afternoon, and night as time passes (you can also use your Digital Crown to move it); you can pick between natural and cityscape landscape. At this writing, the landscapes include: Mack Lake, New York, Hong Kong, London, Paris, and Shanghai.

Photos

The best watch face for last in many people's opinion: photos. Photos lets you show a slideshow of photos and the time. So every time you lift your wrist, something new awaits. Live photos even have animations!

To add this face, swipe all the way to the left of all the watch faces, and then tap New.

Now scroll down to Photos, and tap once.

If you want to show only one particular photo, then open the Photos app on your watch.

84 | Apple Watch Series 5 For Seniors

Scroll to the photo you want. In the photo below, you'll see an icon in the lower right corner of a circle with dots—this indicates that the photo is a live photo and will be animated as an Apple Watch face.

Once it's on the screen, firm press. This will bring up an option to make it the watch face.

You can make it a normal watch face, or an abstract one (kaleidoscope).

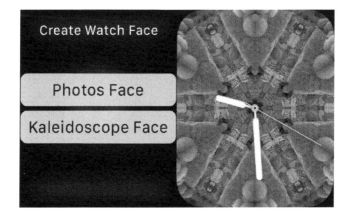

If you want to remove a watch face, just go to change the face as you normally would and swipe up.

[7] Show Me What This Watch Is Capable Of…But Keep It Ridiculously Simple

This chapter will cover:
- Sending / receiving messages
- Reading / sending email
- Using Siri
- Making phone calls
- Adding calendar events
- Setting reminders
- Using the map
- Using photos

- Listening to music
- Looking up the weather
- Setting alarms and timers
- Using the Apple Watch with the Apple TV
- Using the Apple Watch as a Walkie-Talkie

Messages

The first thing you should know about Messages is this isn't the place to type an epic love note. It's the place where you send quick replies. Technically you could do something a little grander, but the time and effort involved makes it rather fruitless.

To begin a new message, go to your watch's Home screen by pressing the knob, tap the Messages icon, and press and hold your finger firmly on the screen. After three seconds it will ask if you'd like to start a new message.

From here, tap Add a Contact. Once you pick your contact, tap Create Message.

There are a few ways you can create a message. The first is to dictate it. When you dictate it, it listens to what you say and transcribes it—not always accurately (especially if it's noisy).

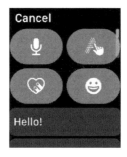

The second way is to scribble it. When you scribble it, you write the letters one at a time. If you need to change a letter, you can delete it, or tap it and scroll through more choices.

Next is the message with taps. This is good if you are trying to get the attention of someone else who is also wearing an Apple Watch. They feel whatever tap vibration you send them.

Finally, you can send an emoji.

Underneath the four ways to create messages are common phrases. Tap any of them and it will add it to the message.

When you receive a message, Apple Watch will tap you. Move your hand toward you and the message will appear automatically; once you put your hand down, it turns off again. Use the watch's side knob to scroll through the message. You'll have the same methods to reply that you did when I showed how to write a message (above).

The biggest difference is Apple Pay is an option now. Apple Pay lets you send money to someone. So if you are out to lunch with a friend, you can pay your share of the bill right from the watch.

If no reply is needed, then hit the Dismiss button instead of the Reply button.

If you are not getting messages on your watch, then chances are a setting is not enabled; you can change the Messages settings from the Apple Watch app on your iPhone.

Reading and Sending Email

When you get mail, you'll get a notification; but there's also an app for reading and managing your email. As it is on the iPhone, the email app is simply named "Mail."

To start, go to the app on your Home screen and tap on it. It looks pretty bare-bones, but there's a lot to it. You can scroll through your messages from within the app. To read a message, tap it.

At any time, you can continue reading the message on your iPhone by swiping up on the Mail icon in the lower left corner of your iPhone's Lock screen. (Note: handoff does need to be set up, so refer to how to set up handoff in this book if you haven't already.)

While Apple Watch does support HTML formats (including different fonts and font colors), it still might look a little off, so for complex messages, the iPhone is the best place to read them.

If it's a long message, you can use the Digital Crown knob to scroll through it.

When a message includes phone numbers or addresses, the watch will automatically recognize them and turn them into hyperlinks. Tapping on them will either bring up the Phone or Map app (depending on what the hyperlink is).

To reply to an email, you will need to use the iPhone to compose it.

Managing Mail

Flag an Email

When you are reading an email on the watch, you can press firmly on the display, and then tap Flag. You can also flag a message from your message list by swiping the message to the left, then tapping on More.

Mark as Unread

If you want to mark a message as unread, go to your message list, swipe left, tap More, and then tap Unread.

Delete an Email

If you want to delete a message, go to your message list, swipe left, tap More, and then tap Trash. (Note: if your email is set up to archive a message, then you'll see the Archive button instead of the Trash button.)

Selecting the Inboxes that Appear

You may not want all of your mail to appear on your watch. Let's say you have a work email, family email, and spam email, and you only want your family email to appear. If that's the case then go to the Apple Watch app on your iPhone, tap My Watch, and then go to Mail and Include Mail. Specify which mailbox you do or do not want to appear.

Customize Alerts

If you want to change how you are alerted when you get mail (or if you don't want alerts at all), then go to the Apple Watch app on your iPhone, and tap My Watch, then turn on Mail Alerts and Show Alerts. "Sound" would be alerts that make noises and "Haptic" is alerts that vibrate.

Message List

If you find your email message list is simply too long, you can reduce the number of lines of the preview by going to the Apple Watch app, tapping on My Watch and then going to Mail and Message Preview; pick two lines of message, one line of message or no lines of a message.

Siri

If you love Siri on the iPhone, you're going to love her even more on your wrist. Don't love her?

Give her a second chance because she got a little bit of an upgrade.

You can access Siri one of two ways (you'll quickly discover that there are multiple ways to do most tasks on the watch):
1. Press the Digital Crown knob.
2. Raise your wrist and speak (say goodbye to "Hey Siri"). Just state your request (e.g. "What's the weather in Paris?" "Who won last night's Yankee game?"); you can use Siri to open apps, set alarms, call friends—pretty much anything you can think of. With no on-board keyboard, Siri is more important than ever.

Making Phone Calls
While you may not go out and buy an Apple Watch to get your Dick Tracy on and make phone calls from your wrist, it's certainly a nice touch…and it's pretty simple to do.

Once your watch is in sync with your iPhone, you are ready to start making and receiving calls.

If a call comes in, you can mute it by placing your hand over the watch. If you want to send it to your phone or reply with a text, then move your finger over the Digital Crown and scroll to the bottom.

To answer the call, use the green button; to decline the call, press the red one. It's just like getting a call on your iPhone. Your watch will use a built-in microphone when you speak into it. It's not the best quality, but it gets the job done.

To make a call, you have two options:

Go to your home screen and tap the Phone icon.

The other option is the easiest; that option is to use Siri. Just lift your wrist and say, "call PERSON'S NAME." If the wrong person is dialed, just hit the Hang Up button and if you do it quickly enough, the call won't go through.

Calendar

The Calendar app on Apple Watch shows events you've scheduled or been invited to today and for the next week. Apple Watch shows events for all calendars you use on your iPhone.

To view your calendar, open the Calendar app on your Home screen; you can also swipe up from your watch face to bring up Glances, and swipe until you get to the Calendar glance. You can also tap on the day's date on the watch face if you've added that option.

You can also see what's going on in your day by lifting your wrist and saying, "Siri, tell me what's going on today."

To switch between the daily events and single list of events, press firmly on the display while you are in the Calendar app, then tap List or Day.

To view a different day, just go to Day view while in the Calendar app, and then swipe left to see the next day's events.

If you want to see the full month, then tap on the '<' in the upper left corner of the Calendar app, and then tap the monthly calendar; repeat the step to go back to Day view. When you are in Month view, any days that you have an activity will be highlighted in red.

Adding Events

To add an event, you will need to open the Calendar app on your iPhone. If you are in the

Calendar app on your watch, then a Calendar icon will appear on your iPhone's Lock screen—just swipe up and it will go immediately to your calendar.

You can have Siri add an event for you.

Responding to Event Invites

When you get an invite to an event, it will appear as a notification; just swipe it or turn the Digital Crown knob when you see it, and then tap Accept, Maybe, or Decline.

The invite will also have the event organizer; to email the event organizer, press firmly on the display while you are looking at the event details; you will be able to either send them a voice message or call them.

To adjust any of your calendar's settings, go to the Apple Watch app on the iPhone, then tap My Watch, and finally tap Calendar.

Reminders

If you use reminders on the iPhone, then you might be disappointed to see there is no Reminders app on the Apple Watch.

Reminders, however, is sort of there; while no app exists, if you create a reminder on your iPhone through the Reminders app, it will also remind you on your watch.

You can also create a reminder on your watch by using Siri; just lift your wrist and say, "Hey Siri, set a reminder."

Map

There are a couple of ways to use the map on your Apple Watch; the first and quickest is to swipe up from your watch face to bring up Glances and then swipe to the Map glance. From here you'll see your current location and what's around you; you can use the Digital Crown knob to zoom in or out. To scroll / pan through the map, use your finger. If you tap the arrow in the bottom left corner, the current location will be updated.

To search the map, tap and hold your finger over the map; this will let you speak what you want to find or see your most recent locations.

You can tap any location that appears on your map to get directions to it or more information about it. You can also stick a pin in an area that you want to go. To add a pin, just touch and hold Map (not firmly) and wait for the pin to drop. If you tap the pin after it's been dropped, it will give you the address. To move the pin, just hover over a new location and drop a new pin. If you aren't sure what someone's address is, if you drop a pin near their location you can get an approximate address.

Directions

Turn-by-turn directions on the Apple Watch is one of the bigger features, and it's really simple to use.

When you get a text with an address, the address is automatically converted to a hyperlink; click on it, and a map will immediately open. You can zoom in and out of the map by turning the Digital Crown knob.

If you don't have a message with the address, then go to your watch's Home screen, tap the Maps icon; the map will appear showing your current location. To find an address, tap your finger firmly on the screen. You'll get an option to either search for the address or use one of your contacts' addresses. When you search for an address, it will give you the option to use a recently used address, or speak the address through dictation.

When the address comes up, there will be two options: driving directions and walking directions. Walking will not only change the time it will take, but also take you down paths a car cannot go. Once you make your selection by tapping, just hit the Start button.

One of the cool features about the map is the turn-by-turn directions. When it's time to make a turn, your watch will tap you to get your attention. Even more cool is if you start directions on your phone, it will also appear on your watch.

Photos

To view photos on the Apple Watch, go to the Photos app on your watch Home screen; because the watch cannot actually take photos, the photos you see will be the ones from your iPhone album. By default, the watch is set to display only your Favorites album, but you can change this.

Once the app is open, just tap the photo you want to view and use the Digital Crown knob to zoom in or out and use your finger to pan. Zoom all the way out to see all of your photos.

Pick an Album

If you'd like to choose another album to show on your watch then open the Apple Watch app on the iPhone and tap My Watch, then go to Photos and Synced Album and pick the album you want to sync; you can also create a new album using photos from your phone.

Storage

The watch does not have as much space as your phone so it's important to limit how much you store on it; to limit photo storage, open the Apple Watch app on the iPhone, tap My Watch, then go to Photos and Photo Limits.

You can see how many photos are currently on your Apple Watch by opening the Settings app from the watch's Home screen, tapping General, and then About. You can also see this on your phone by opening the Apple Watch app, then tapping My Watch, General, and About.

Camera Viewfinder

While the watch doesn't have a camera built in, it does have a pretty awesome feature that lets you use the watch as an external camera viewfinder and shutter to your iPhone camera.

For this to work, you need to make sure the watch is no more than 30 ft. from your iPhone.

To take a photo, open the Camera app on your watches Home screen, then position the iPhone to frame the shot using the Apple Watch as your viewfinder. If you want to change the exposure, just tap the area you want to focus on from your Apple Watch preview; tap the shutter button on your watch. You can preview the photo on your watch, but the photo will actually be saved on the iPhone.

Next to the shutter button is a timer button; if you want to do a timed shot, tap that; the timer takes burst shots, which is great for action / sports photos.

Music

The Music app is, of course, on your Home screen, but you can reach it more quickly by swiping up on your screen.

Like almost anything on the watch, you can also play music with Siri. Just lift your wrist and say, "play Bob Dylan."

When music is playing, tap the top corner and you'll have the option to scroll through Artist, Albums, Playlist and Songs (scroll using the Digital Crown knob).

The watch automatically syncs to your phone and will play music that's on your iPhone. That's great when your phone is nearby, but sometimes you don't have your phone nearby and want to listen to music directly on your watch. You can load music to your watch pretty easily.

To add music, connect your watch to its charger, then open the Apple Watch app on your iPhone. Next, tap Music (it's near the bottom). After that, tap Sync Playlist, and choose the songs you want to add.

To play music directly from your watch, open the Music app and press firmly on the screen when the app opens. This will open a new menu with four options: Shuffle, Repeat, Source, and Airplay. Select Source. Next select Apple Watch. It will now walk you through pairing your watch with Bluetooth headsets to listen to the music.

From the previous menu, you can also select Airplay to pair your watch with an Airplay enabled speaker.

Stocks

If you'd like to monitor one or more stocks from your watch, open the Stocks app; you can see details about a stock by tapping it in the list and then turning the Digital Crown to scroll.

You can also use Siri to find a stock price by saying, "What was the closing price for XYZ stock?"

You can also see stocks as a glance by swiping up from your watch face, and swiping to the Stocks glance. From here you can also add stocks.

Weather

There are a couple of ways to check weather on your watch; one of the easiest is to swipe up from your watch face to bring up Glances, and then find the Weather glance.

If you want more detailed weather information, then go to the Weather app by opening it on the watch Home screen. The Weather app will have the 10-day forecast, current temperature and conditions, and chance of rain.

The Weather app is synced to your iPhone, so if you want to add or remove a city, then do it from your phone.

You can change the default city being shown on your watch by opening the Apple Watch app on your iPhone, tapping on My Watch, and then going to Weather and Default City.

Activity

One of the features that Apple is really promoting with the Apple Watch is Activity; one of the reasons to wear the watch, if you are to believe Apple, is to get you to move more. It's a hard sell with me, because I'm a lazy bum!

The app is divided up into three fitness goals: stand up for at least one minute of every hour, hit your calorie burn goal by moving more (you can set your goal), and accumulate 30 minutes of an activity that requires movement above a brisk walk. Each of these goals make up rings; as you complete your goals, the rings begin to fill up, and by the end of the day they should ideally be full.

To get started, go to your Home screen and tap the Activity app. The first time that you open the app, it will give you a very short tutorial on what the app is and how it helps you live a happier, healthier life. Once you finish the tutorial, you'll have to enter some personal information—this is for your eyes only and you only do it once. It will help ensure the app is as accurate as possible. For each section, turn the Digital Crown to enter your information.

After you've finished, you will indicate your activity level; you can change this later, so if you aren't sure, then go for lower—not higher. Next you'll see your suggested goal, which you can accept or adjust. When you are done, tap Start Moving. Your app will now be tracking you in the background. There's no need to start anything each day.

You can access the Activity app at any time by tapping on it from your Home screen. The first thing you'll see is all the rings together. You can use your Digital Crown to see more detailed information on the rings.

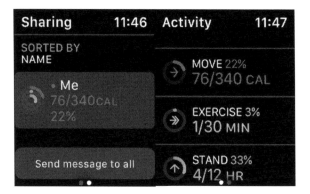

At any time, you can change your goals by opening the app, then pressing firmly on the display. You can also have reminders sent to you to encourage you to complete your goals.

In the Activity app on your iPhone, you can view your Activity history, and see more detailed reports about what you've done. The measurements will get more accurate as you wear the watch more and it gets to know your behaviors.

Finally, if you swipe left on the Activity app, you can share your activity goals; perfect for the lazy bum like me, who likes to remind his spouse that they were sitting around all day.

Workout

Workout is kind of a companion to Activity even though there's a separate app for it. The point of it is to help you track progress during a workout session and help you hit new milestones.

From your Home screen, tap the Workout app and you'll immediately see dozens of different workouts. They range from brisk walks to more intense workouts—both indoor and outdoor. For indoor and outdoor running or walking and outdoor cycling, you can also set a distance goal. You can also choose no goal and simply get started.

The following are some of the workouts you can choose from:
- Outdoor walk
- Outdoor run
- Outdoor cycle
- Indoor walk
- Indoor run
- Indoor cycle
- Elliptical
- Rower
- Stair stepper
- High intensity interval training (HIIT)
- Hiking

- Yoga
- Pool swim
- Open water swim
- Other (no, this isn't where you track the fitness goal "watch TV")

You can either start the workout or set goals. To set a goal (such as how far you want to walk), tap the three dots.

This will bring up four options: Open, Calories, Distance, and Time.

What these options will do is set a goal. So, as an example, let's say my goal is to walk three miles; I add three miles, then tap Begin, and it will start tracking. I'll get alerted when I hit three miles.

Once you hit Begin, the watch will immediately count down to start. During your workout, a ring will steadily fill in here as you approach your goal.

To pause or end the workout, just press firmly on the display and press End or Pause. When you end the workout, you can scroll through a full summary. You can either save the data or discard it.

Check Your Heart Rate

To get the best results with your heart rate, make sure the watch is tight enough to touch the skin, but not too tight.

It will measure your heart rate when you load the app.

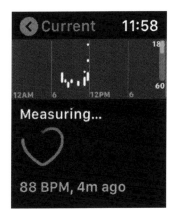

Tapping on any of the three options: Current, Resting Rate, or Walking Average, will get you an overview of your heart rate.

 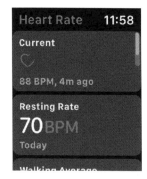

If you are in a workout, you can check your heart rate by swiping on the lower half of the Workout progress screen.

Cycle Tracking

Cycle tracking isn't an app, rather it's a new feature in the Health app of your watch. It tracks your menstrual cycle and can help predict when your next period will come or when your fertile window is about to start. (Pay careful attention to that word "prediction"! The watch should obviously not be used as a form of birth control.)

To get started, put down your watch and open up your phone. Open the Health app, then go to Cycle Tracking and select Get Started.

Follow the instructions and make sure and add the features you want (such as Period Prediction and Fertility Prediction).

Once your information is added, you can now start logging things like your flow level or other symptoms.

Set Alarms

If you want to set an alarm, go to the Alarm Clock app from your watch's Home screen.

Once it's open, press firmly on the display, then tap Add Alarm. Tap Change Time (remember to also change AM / PM); you can use the Digital Crown knob to adjust the hours and minutes. Finally tap Set. You can tap the '<' in the upper left corner to return to the alarm settings, where you can repeat an alarm, push snooze, or label it.

To adjust an alarm, tap the Alarm Clock app, then tap the alarm in the list that you want to change. Tap next to the alarm to turn it on or off. You can delete an alarm by tapping on the alarm, then scrolling to the bottom and tapping Delete.

Use a Timer

To use the watch's timer, go to the Home screen and tap Timer; timers can be set for up to 24 hours. To set a timer, open the app, tap hours or minutes, turn the Digital Crown knob to adjust the time, and finally tap Start. If the timer will be more than 12 hours, then while adjusting the timer press firmly on the display and tap 0-24 hours.

Use the Stopwatch

If you want to use the stopwatch to time things like the time of a track lap, then go to your Home screen and tap the Stopwatch app. To start the watch, tap the Start button; tap the Lap button to split the time or record a lap. Timing will continue as you switch between them. When you are finished, tap Reset.

You can also pick the format for the stopwatch; there are four different ones: Analog, Digital, Graph, and Hybrid.

Audiobooks

Apple has not yet put their popular Books app on the Apple Watch—probably because reading is just not a great experience on the watch. There are third-party apps that do this if it's a must-have feature. What Apple offers in the place of a native bookstore is the ability to listen to audiobooks that you purchased from the Apple Books store.

It's a pretty straightforward app; scroll to the audiobook that you want and tap it.

From here, you can play the book, or fast-forward / rewind. The '1x' in the lower right corner adjusts the playback speed, so you can have the narrator read faster.

Calculator

Simple calculations could be performed on the watch by using Siri in earlier versions of the Apple Watch, but a native app was missing. Many people are surprised it took so long to get this app on the watch. Whatever the reason for the wait, it's here now, and it does more than you might expect.

116 | *Apple Watch Series 5 For Seniors*

In addition to basic calculations there's a Tip button. This helps you quickly see how much of a tip you should leave. Type in the cost, then tap the Tip button. You can use the Digital Crown to adjust the percentage.

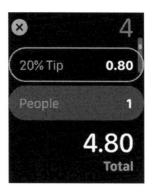

Tap the People button below the percentage and you can split the bill. Use the Digital Crown to adjust how many people are with you. As you add people, it will show the cost for each person below the final price.

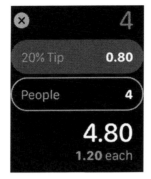

Remote Control

A lesser-known fact about the watch is that it doubles as a remote control for iTunes and Apple TV.

Before you begin, make sure both your watch and your device are using the same network; if your phone is using one Wi-Fi and your watch is using another, then they won't work.

Remote Play iTunes

If you'd like to use the watch as a remote for iTunes on your Mac, open up the Remote app; next tap the Add Device (+).

In iTunes on your computer, click the Remote button near the top of the iTunes window; it will ask you to enter the 4-digit code that is now displayed on your watch. (Note: if you look for the Remote button in iTunes before you tap Add Device on the Apple Watch, you'll be waiting a long time—it will only appear after you tap Add Device; also make sure iTunes is up-to-date.)

Remote for Apple TV

If you'd like to use the watch as a remote for iTunes on your Apple TV, open up the Remote app; next tap the Add Device (+). (Note: remember you must be using the same Wi-Fi Network.)

On your Apple TV go to Settings, and then General, and finally Remote, and select the Apple Watch; enter the passcode that's currently on your watch.

Walkie-Talkie

WatchOS 5 made it a whole lot easier to communicate with those close by with its Walkie-Talkie feature. WatchOS 6 keeps this feature. To use it, both people need to have an Apple Watch Series 1 or later and WatchOS 6. You also need to turn on FaceTime because you will be using FaceTime Audio.

Unfortunately, this feature is not available in all countries.

The first time you use the app, you will need to add friends. Open the app. Tap ⊕, then choose a contact.

Now wait. It's not like a phone call where it connects right away with your friend. They have to give you permission to reach them. It will stay gray until the person accepts. Once they accept you can start talking away instantly.

To remove a friend, open the Walkie-Talkie app, swipe left on the friend, then tap ✕. Or open the Apple Watch app on your iPhone, tap Walkie-Talkie > Edit, tap ⊖, then tap Remove.

To start a conversation, just open the app, tap the friend's name (after they've accepted), and wait for it to connect (they have to be wearing the watch). Once connected, tap Talk and say something, then let go when you are done.

You can turn the volume up and down with the Digital Crown.

If you no longer want to talk over this feature, just open it and toggle it to off; if a contact tries to reach you, it will say you are unavailable.

If you turn on Silent mode, you can still hear the person's voice and the chimes that come in. If you turn on Theater mode or Do Not Disturb then it will make you unavailable to talk.

[8]
WHAT OTHER THINGS SHOULD I KNOW ABOUT THE APPLE WATCH?

This chapter will cover:
- Accessibility features
- How to care for the Apple Watch
- How to reset the Apple Watch
- How to update the Apple Watch

Like every Apple product, the Apple Watch has accessibility features to help people with disabilities.

It works very similarly to your iPhone; to access the features, go to the Apple Watch app on your iPhone, then My Watch, then General, and finally Accessibility.

VoiceOver

VoiceOver helps you use the watch even if you can't see the watch. It will read back everything that's on the watch for you. You can turn it on by going to the Settings app on the watch's Home screen, then General, Accessibility, and finally VoiceOver.

When VoiceOver is on, you can move your finger around the display and listen to the name of each item you touch. VoiceOver also uses different gestures; you can go back by using two fingers to draw a "Z" shape on the display. To open an app, you will double tap it instead of single tap. To pause the VoiceOver from reading what's on the screen, tap the display with two fingers; tap with two fingers again to resume play.

When you set up your watch for the first time, you can use VoiceOver as well. When you turn on the watch for the first time, press the side button; after it turns on, triple click the Digital Crown knob.

Zoom

The watch is a small display—perhaps even smaller than you thought it would be—so it's understandable that you might want the display a little bigger. If that's the case, go to the Settings app, and then turn on General, Accessibility, and Zoom.

To zoom in or out when Zoom is enabled you will double tap the display with two fingers. To move around (or pan) the display, you will drag with two fingers.

Bold Text

Putting the text in boldface is another way to make reading the text on your screen a little easier. You can make the text boldface by going to the Settings app on your Home screen, then tapping General and Accessibility and turning on Bold Text; the watch will need to be restarted before this goes into effect.

Handling

Removing the Bands

To change a band, press the band release button on the Apple Watch and slide the band across, then slide in the new band. You should never force a band into the slot, as this could get it stuck.

It is recommended that you fit the band so it is close to your skin, but not so tight that it is squeezing your wrist.

Band Care

Apple recommends that you clean the leather portions of bands with a nonabrasive, lint-free cloth that is, if necessary, dampened with water. The band should not be attached to the watch while cleaning. After cleaning, let the band dry before re-attaching to the watch. Do not store leather in direct sunlight, or in high temperatures or high humidity; you also should not soak the leather in water as it is not water resistant.

For all other bands, Apple recommends cleaning the same way, but the band should be dried with a nonabrasive, lint-free cloth.

A Little More Advanced

Force Restarting the Apple Watch

In very rare cases, the Apple Watch may freeze or need to be force restarted. If this ever happens, hold down the side button and Digital Crown knob at the same time for ten seconds. When the Apple logo appears, you can let go.

Resetting the Watch Settings

If you want to reset the watch settings and make the watch like new (remember this erases everything), then go to the Settings app from the Home screen, then go to General, Reset, and finally Erase All Content and Settings. Once it's reset you will need to pair it with your phone again. Make sure you do this if you ever sell or give your watch or phone away, as your vital information (like credit cards) will be available to that person if you don't.

Get Your Watch DNA

If you need to know what model number your watch is, what software version it is, what its serial number is, or what its capacity is then go to the Settings app from your Home screen, and then General and About.

Update Apple Watch Software

Much like the iPhone and iPad, updates to the Apple Watch software are done over the air—meaning you won't need to plug anything in.

To see if there's an update, open the Apple Watch app on the iPhone, then tap My Watch, General, and finally Software Updates. It will tell you if there's an update, and then you just follow the steps. Updates don't happen very often—usually just a handful of times each year.

[9] So Many Bands and Accessories, So Little Time

> This chapter will cover:
> - Official Apple Watch bands and accessories

Watch Bands & Accessories

What's a watch without its band? Unlike traditional bands, the Apple Watch makes it remarkably easy to switch out bands. And unlike any other Apple product, you have lots of options; normally an Apple product comes in two or three colors, but with the watches there are several dozen ways to mix and match.

Below is a guide to all the different options you have to choose from. (Note: when purchasing a band, remember that a 42mm band won't be compatible with a 38mm watch or vice versa.) Unless otherwise noted, all bands are available in both 38 and 42mm. Some bands are not one size fits all.

Official Bands & Accessories

Sport Band

It's available in black, space gray, white, pink, blue, and green. The band is obviously best for working out; it's also the cheapest band available. It's made of fluoroelastomer, a synthetic rubber known for performing well in heat. Because this band isn't one size fits all, the chart below helps you make the right choice:

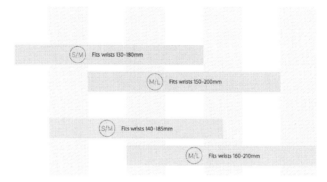

Classic Buckle

This band is made of Dutch leather from a tannery in the Netherlands. Apple promises the mill gives it a distinctive texture. The closer is made of stainless steel.

Milanese Loop

Apple says the inspiration for this stainless-steel mesh band was a mesh band from 19th century Milan. The band is completely magnetic and easy to put on.

Modern Buckle
Three sizes: small, medium, and large.

It's available in brown, black, pink, and midnight blue. The leather for this stunning band comes from a French tannery established in 1803. How are the modern and classic bands different? The leather is slightly different, but the most noticeable difference is the buckle. The classic is a strap with holes; the modern is a magnetic band that helps you have a more precise fit. Because this band isn't one size fits all, the chart below helps you make the right choice:

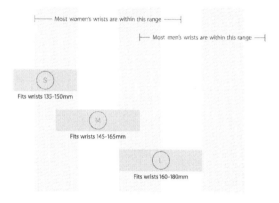

Link Bracelet

One of the most expensive and complex bands, this stainless-steel band has over 100 parts. Apple claims the craftsmanship is so complex that it takes nine hours to assemble a single case. The magnetic closure is one size fits all.

Leather Loop
Only available for the 42mm band.

It's available in stone, light brown, bright blue, and black. Made of Venezia leather and hand-crafted in Arzignano, Italy, this band has a soft and gilded feel. The magnetic loop is easy to put on. Because this band isn't one size fits all, the chart below helps you make the right choice:

Apple Watch Magnetic Charging Cable
($29 for 1m cable; $39 for 2m cable)

Apple has only announced one official accessory for the Apple Watch, and that is an extra charger (one comes free with your watch).

[10]
ACCESSIBILITY

> This chapter will cover:
> - Changing accessibility features from your watch
> - Changing accessibility features from your phone

As you probably know by now, most things on the Apple Watch can be configured both on the watch and the phone. That's true for accessibility features...kind of. While it is true that you can adjust some accessibility features right on the watch, you cannot adjust all of them.

To get started, I'll first show you how to do it on the Apple Watch; next, I'll show you how you can do even more by using your phone.

Accessibility is located in Settings. To get started, go to your Home screen on the watch, then tap the Settings icon. It looks like the below icon:

From here, scroll until you see General.

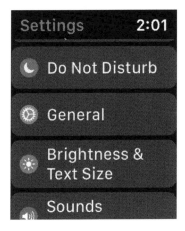

Next select accessibility.

There are four different options you can pick from.

- VoiceOver
- Zoom
- Reduce Motion
- On/Off labels

To activate any of them, just tap on them and toggle them on. Before doing so, however, let's go over what each one does when you tap on them.

All of these features work essentially the same way as they will on your phone.

Starting with VoiceOver, the watch will dictate what's on your screen when you tap it. This changes the functionality of the watch a little. To select something you swipe left or right; to activate something, you double tap.

There are things on the watch, like photos, that can be zoomed in; if you want to be able to zoom in on everything, then activate this by tapping the switch toggle; to zoom, double-tap with two fingers (not one) and rotate your Digital Crown to adjust the view.

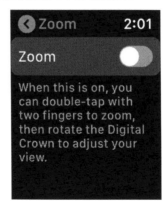

Motion is something some people like, others don't notice, and some get dizzy with. If you are of the latter, then this toggle turns it on or off. If you find that things are moving too much on your screen, switch it off and see if you like the experience better.

The last option is pretty straight-forward: it turns labels on and off.

Now, let's go to your phone where there are even more Apple Watch accessibility features.

There are two settings on your phone: one for your phone and one for your watch. To get to the one on your watch, open the Watch app. Next, scroll to "General."

From here, tap Accessibility.

You'll now see a lot more things you can control than what you see on your watch.

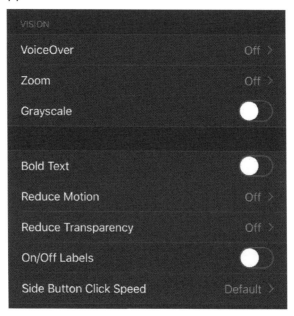

Changes to the watch happen pretty instantly—so fast you might not even notice. So, for example, if you tap Zoom on your phone, the change is already made by the time you finish this sentence. There's no Save or any button to make it take effect.

I've already covered the first two options in this menu (VoiceOver and Zoom); they work exactly the same from your phone as your watch, but they have a lot more options on your phone.

Starting with VoiceOver, when you tap it on your iPhone, you'll see a menu to adjust the speed rate of the voice speaking back, as well as Screen Curtain, which has VoiceOver working even though the screen is turned off.

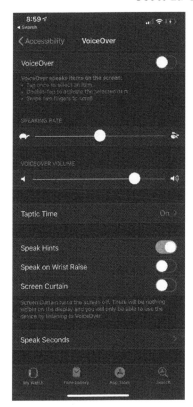

On the watch, Zoom is pretty simple: it zooms! On the phone, you can be more specific and adjust how much you want to zoom. So, if you only want things a little bit bigger you can lessen the amount of the zoom.

Grayscale is new and it does what it sounds like: changes the color on your watch to greyscale. Everything on your phone (even photos) will have no colors.

The next four options don't have menus—they're just on/off toggles. They do exactly what they say: make things bolder, reduce the motion, turn off/on labels, and reduce the transparency.

The last point on transparency hasn't been covered, but it's pretty straight-forward. There are a few things that have a layer of transparency that makes it harder to read. This option reduces that if you are struggling.

As I've mentioned, there are only two buttons on the Apple Watch. The round one that turns (the Digital Crown) and the long one (the Side Button).

Chances are you are completely comfortable with the speed of the Side Button. If you find it's too difficult to press it quickly, this option slows it down.

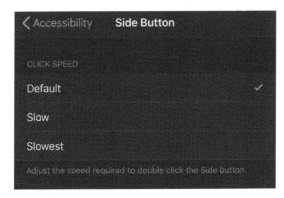

If you are using a wheelchair, then you wouldn't want to track your number of steps—but that's not to say you can't still use the watch for fitness. If you want to set up the watch for wheelchair use, then you won't do it here. You go into the Health section. Hit the back button above (it looks like this: <General). This only brings you to the General menu, so you'll want to go back one more screen, then open up health.

Setting up Wheelchair is greyed out; there's a button on top that says Edit. Tap that and you can now adjust it. It's a simple yes or no question.

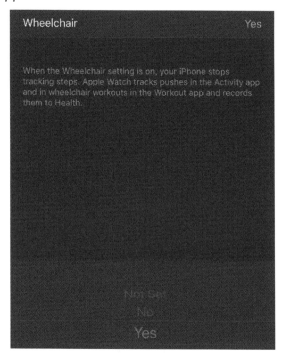

Going back to accessibility, there are some options for hearing. The sound on the watch is in stereo, which means it evenly comes out of all channels. You can set it to mono (two channels), and further adjust if you want more sound out of one channel or the other. This works great if you have headphones in and want more sound to come to your left ear than right, for example.

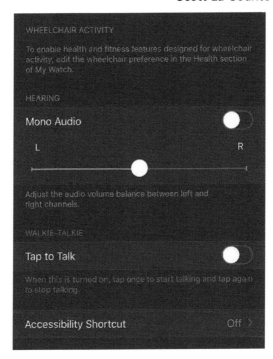

Finally, there's an option for shortcuts. This turns the Digital Crown's triple-click on. When you push your Digital Crown three times, for example, it would zoom in—or turn on VoiceOver.

ABOUT THE AUTHOR

Scott La Counte is a librarian and writer. His first book, *Quiet, Please: Dispatches from a Public Librarian* (Da Capo 2008) was the editor's choice for the Chicago Tribune and a Discovery title for the Los Angeles Times; in 2011, he published the YA book The N00b Warriors, which became a #1 Amazon bestseller; his most recent book is *#OrganicJesus: Finding Your Way to an Unprocessed, GMO-Free Christianity* (Kregel 2016).

He has written dozens of best-selling how-to guides on tech products.

You can connect with him at ScottDouglas.org.

Printed in Great Britain
by Amazon